MW00345069

THREE LEGS GOOD

THE STORY BEHIND THE MANX TRISKELION

SARA GOODWINS

HOOFPRINT SERIES 3

Loaghtan Books
Caardee
Dreemskerry Hill
Maughold
Isle of Man
IM7 1BE

Published by Loaghtan Books

First published: March 2015

Copyright © Sara Goodwins, 2015

Typesetting and origination by:
Loaghtan Books

Printed and bound by:
Geerings Print Ltd

Website: www.loaghtanbooks.com

ISBN: 978 1 908060 11 2

Photographic copyright © George Hobbs, 2015
unless otherwise stated

All rights reserved. No part of this publication may be reproduced, stored on a retrieval system or transmitted in any form or by any means without prior permission of the publishers.

In memory of the *real* Captain Tripod

Hoofprint series

Front cover: *Triskelion on Ballaterson farmhouse, Maughold*

Rear cover: *Gnomen of a sundial at Holy Trinity church, Kirk Patrick*

Title page: *Stained glass window, church of St Brigit, Kirk Bride. Spot the triskelion!*

Contents page: *Plaque on the office of the Isle of Man Harbour Commissioners, Peel*

CONTENTS

LEGENDS OR LEG-ENDS?

The pub was warm and cosy, many locals gathered round
To discuss their nationality and the problems they had found:
'When visiting', cried one of them, 'folks think that I'm a Scot'
'Or English', said another, 'in fact everything I'm not.'
They all agreed but could not think how these mistakes to quash,
While a tabby cat sat by the fire and gave his paws a wash.
His name was Captain Tripod, he was an old Manx cat;
Some years before he'd lost a leg in battle with a rat.
He'd earned his bed beside the fire and, snoozing in his place,
Was still an able mouser and well worthy of his race.
A stranger listened to the talk; he was old and closely cloaked,
Despite protective clothing his hair and beard were soaked.
They welcomed him beside the fire, he gave a nod of thanks,
And said: 'you need a symbol to let people know you're Manx.'
He pointed to his leggings, and the stool on which he sat,
The golden firelight, blood-red wine, and even to the cat.
'Three legs in armour's right for you, united, all for one.
Put them against a bright red flag and shape them like the sun.
For motto, let it state the Manx are tough and love their land:
"No matter what you do to me, you know that I shall stand".'
Each looked at each and nodded; they were pleased and none said nay,
And, while they were agreeing, old Manannan slipped away.

And that's why Mann has got three legs, joined, balanced on their toes:
They represent the island… Or so the story goes.

THE SYMBOL AND ITS HISTORY

The Three Legs of Man is a variation of the triskele or triskelion. The word means 'three legged' and is a name usually given to a pattern consisting of three lines or legs identically bent or curved and joined at one end. Such patterns are often associated with Celtic art, although they existed far earlier than the Celts and appear in many cultures including those of Greece, Mycenae and North America.

Older than Stonehenge

Some of the earliest examples of triskelia in the British Isles are at Brú na Bóinne (sometimes called Newgrange), County Meath in Ireland. The site is Neolithic – which means new stone age – and about 5,000 years old. It's therefore older than both Stonehenge and the Pyramids. Brú na Bóinne consists mainly of a huge circular mound, 76 metres across (about the same area as a football pitch) and 12 metres high (roughly the height of the terminal building at Ronaldsway airport). The mound has a long passageway leading to a single central chamber. At the entrance to the passageway is a large stone decorated with spiral triskelia and in the central chamber a spiral triskelion, about a foot square, has been carved on the wall. Above the entrance doorway is another small opening through which the sun shines at the winter solstice illuminating the central chamber and lighting the triskelion.

Tri-spiral in the central chamber of Brú na Bóinne. Photograph courtesy of The Office of Public Works in Ireland

No-one knows why the huge mound was originally built, although given its position and the annual illumination of the tri-spiral it seems clear that the area had a ritual significance and was something to do with the sun at midwinter. It also seems a reasonable deduction that the triskelia are more than mere decoration, but are symbolic of a belief system vital to the stone age builders and designers.

Bronze age Celtic coin, known as a 'rainbow cup' because it forms a shallow dish like a saucer. It was thought to be the 'gold' at the end of the rainbow, as hoards were sometimes found when ploughing

Connexions to the Celts...

Brú na Bóinne was not the only culture which stressed the importance of spirals. Archaeological finds at La Tène in Neuchâtel, Switzerland, Hochdorf and der Enz in Baden-Württemberg, Germany, and Battersea in London, England all use swirls and spirals in their decoration and have become very strongly associated with Celtic art.

Interestingly, Brú na Bóinne in County Meath is just north of Dublin, which makes it one of the closest part of Ireland to the Isle of Man; Mann has always been very strongly influenced by Ireland and its culture, particularly early in the two countries' history. The triskelion is one of the two symbols which represent Manannan mac Lir

– the other is the trident as 'mac Lir' means 'son of the sea'. Manannan is the legendary protector of the Isle of Man, and the god after whom the island is traditionally named.

... and Achilles

Having been carved 5,000 years ago at Brú na Bóinne, the next appearance of the triskelion in history is in Ancient Greece where it seems to have had some connexion with Achilles. Around 500 BC a triskelion appears on Greek pottery and coinage. The three-legged symbol, joined at waist level, higher than would be the case now, and without clothing, is displayed as an heraldic device on a shield carried by Achilles. It is depicted

DID YOU KNOW?

The number three is a prime number (which is a number divisible only by itself and 1) so is very important to mathematicians.

on a vase now in the Boston museum in the US (see picture, left). The shield of Achilles is described in Homer's *Iliad* as having 'the earth upon it, and the sky, and the sea's water, and the tireless sun, and the moon waxing into her fullness, and on it all the constellations that festoon the heavens…' (*Iliad*, book 18, lines 483-5, Lattimore translation). The *Iliad* is thought to have been composed around 750 BC so would have been well known to the artist who decorated the vase – rather as we know Shakespeare today. Could the three-legged symbol he used somehow represent the whole of the known universe? It is also interesting that it is definitely legs which are pictured, not merely spiral lines. When and why the change was made we don't know.

From a vase to coinage. Around 200 years after the symbol appeared on the Achilles vase, it turns up on coins from Syracuse, which is a city and province in Sicily. The drachma (see picture, right) dates from around 315 BC. The feet on the unclothed legs are now winged and a face appears at the centre of the triskelion, where the legs join. The emblem on the modern Sicilian flag (see picture on page 14) is almost identical. The face is usually taken to be that of Medusa but is sometimes said to be Persephone. Medusa was a gorgon with snakes for hair who turned people into stone if they looked into her eyes; Persephone personified crops and was carried off by Hades from Enna, a central town in Sicily, to become the queen of the underworld.

Winged feet are often associated with Hermes (the Roman god Mercury) who was the herald and messenger of the gods and wore winged sandals for speed, while Mercury is sometimes associated with the Celtic god Lugus. Some experts think that Lugus was a trinity god, with three distinct characters; a triskelion would therefore be a particularly appropriate symbol for such a deity. Interestingly, the trophy awarded to senior race winners in the Manx TT features a statuette of Mercury.

Although the three legs on the Syracusean coin on the bottom of the previous page are naked and winged, their shape is very reminiscent of the armoured and spurred Three Legs of Man, and a possible forerunner of it.

Silver coin from Syracuse, Sicily, c 300 BC. The standing figure is probably Nike, the Greek goddess of victory, holding a trophy of arms

Looking East

Other cultures liked triskelia too; the symbol appears in several Asian countries and cultures. In Japan a *tomoe* is a decorative symbol which looks something like a comma. A *mitsudomoe* is a three-fold tomoe, where the three 'commas' form a circle around each other; the gap between them looks like a triskelion (see picture, right). The three elements of the mitsudomoe are sometimes taken to represent the three divisions of the Shinto religion, which are man, earth and sky. Shinto is a very old religion, founded according to tradition in the seventh century BC, although written records do not begin until over a millennium later. The mitsudomoe was associated with Hachiman, the Shinto god of warriors, and through Hachiman was occasionally adopted by samurai. Consequently many Japanese families use mitsudomoe as a kind of family crest or seal today.

West of Japan, Buddhists, particularly those of Tibet, use a variation of a triskelion called a *gankyil* or 'circle of bliss'. Looking very like a mitsudomoe but without the gap in the centre, the word gankyil comes from the Lhasan words *dga* meaning 'total happiness' or 'joy', and *khyil* meaning 'circle' or 'wheel'. To Buddhists the wheel represents primordial energy, while the circle can also stand for the three jewels which are the heart of the Buddhist ideals. The jewels are red for Buddha, blue for *Dharma* (teaching), and yellow for *Sangha* (the community of the enlightened). Buddhism is another very old religion, beginning in Nepal in the 6th century BC. In Korea the same shape is known as *Sam Saeg-ui Taegeuk* and the blue, red and yellow represent respectively heaven, earth and people, and the way they influence each other.

Whatever its meaning to various believers, the triskelion symbol seems to have had the same fate as some of the holy sites of the older faiths. Just as the Christian church took over sites of pagan worship, so it also seems to have taken over the use of older symbols. The fish, for example, came to mean Christ but had previously been associated with goddesses of fertility such as the Roman Venus and Egyptian Isis. Similarly the triskelion, from being a pagan symbol began to be used to represent the Christian trinity of God the Father, God the Son and God the Holy Spirit. Today the triskelion has been adopted as a spiritual symbol by both Christian and pagan believers. In different ways it stands for the sun, the cycle of life, earth/sea/sky, eternity and therefore God.

The three horns of Odin

The Celts were not the only major influence on Manx culture, as invading Vikings brought their own beliefs – and the symbols of it – with them.

Triskelia seem to have been important to the Norsemen too and various forms appear on Viking carvings and runestones. One of the favoured versions of a triskelion is sometimes called the three horns of Odin. The symbol consists of three interlocked stylized drinking horns and refers to a legend about Odin, leader of the Norse gods, and his quest for magical mead. As is often the case in folk tales the details vary, but the mead was said to have been brewed from the blood of a wise man called Kvasir, who kept it in three drinking horns the names of which were Óðrœrir, Boðn and Són. Over three days Odin bargained with the giantess Gunnlöð to be allowed to drink from each horn and so gained wisdom and poetic inspiration.

Experts think that the three-horns symbol indicates wisdom, learning and poetical skill – presumably the particular properties of Óðrœrir, Boðn and Són. The symbol appears, for example, to the right of the horseman's head on one of the Gotland runestones, the Stenkyrka stone, Lillebjärs, Sweden (see picture, left) as well as on the Snoldelev runestone, Ramsø, Denmark, both from the ninth century. As the name implies, runestones have runes carved on them. The runes on the Snodlelev stone say: *kunualts stain sunar ruhalts þular o salhaukum* (Gunwald's stone, Hróaldr's son, reciter of Salhaugar). Calling Gunwald a 'reciter' is unusual and indicates that he's some sort of orator, either a poet/bard or possibly a priest or lawgiver. The three-horned symbol would be particularly appropriate for a bard.

On the Stenkyrka stone (opposite page), to the left of the horseman's head is another important 'sign of three' for Norsemen: three interlocking triangles. Modern experts refer to the symbol as a valknut – no-one knows what the Vikings called it – from the Old Norse *valr* meaning 'warriors killed in battle' and *knut* meaning 'knot'. Although not strictly a triskelion, the valknut shares the three-fold symbolism. Unfortunately we don't really know what the valknut represents or signifies. Its position indicates that it's more than just decoration, and it usually appears in pictures where someone is about to be killed. Odin, or symbols referring to him, also often appear with or near a valknut. The best we can do is to assume that the emblem is symbolic of the circle of life into death.

A knotty problem

Visually the valknut is very like the triquetra, and a triquetra might be where the shape of the Three Legs of Man comes from. The triquetra is a simple design made of three semi-circles which can be drawn without the pencil leaving the page – try it; you'll find it's quite easy to do. If however the triquetra is designed as a rope formed into the knot and tied tightly, the central section is exactly the shape of the Three Legs of Man (see picture above).

One of the Funbo runestones now at Uppsala University, Sweden. A triquetra appears in the centre, while the runes in the serpent around the circumference say: þegn ok gunnarr reistu steina eptir veðr bróður sinn *(Thane and Gunnar raised this stone for Vethr, their brother)*

Triquetra appear fairly frequently on Scandinavian runestones and also on eighth-century Manx crosses. The Mal Lumkun Cross at Kirk Michael (see picture, left), a fragment of a cross slab found at Santon, and the famous Calf of Man cross, for example, all carry triquetra designs. Like the triskelion the triquetra was also adopted by the Christian church as a symbol of the three-fold nature of God, and is now often called the trinity knot. Also like the triskelion, the triquetra continues to be used as a symbol in the pagan faiths.

Respectability – and infamy

Triskelia or tri-spirals are said to resemble the sun, but are not the only radiating patterns which do so. Four rather than three lines is at least as common. Often called sun crosses, four-legged symbols are frequently variants of a vertical cross within a circle. Shapes such as the Armenian *arevakhach*, (see picture, right) and the swastika were all originally sun symbols.

It's thought that the swastika began as a sun cross, before the circle was broken to form the right angled 'legs'. The circular pattern may then have developed into a square, as straight lines are easier to draw and carve – a swastika is carved above the three horn symbol on the Snoldelev runestone in Denmark, mentioned on page 8 – and is certainly easier to fit into items such as tiles in pavements. The earliest swastika dates from 10,000 BC and was carved onto mammoth ivory in the Ukraine.

In Europe one of the earliest forms of the swastika was probably the *lauburu*, from the Basque *lau* meaning 'flat', 'even' or 'four' and *buru* meaning 'head' or 'chief', hence 'four heads' (see picture, right). Tradition says that the Basques have been using the symbol since the second century BC, but it seems to have become popular in the sixteenth century when Spain was nervous of cultural independence and tried to impose conformity, often by armed repression.

The swastika symbol was certainly widely used in the Bronze age and is still used as a sacred symbol in Eastern religions including Hinduism and Buddhism – it occasionally appeared decorating Rudyard Kipling's Indian writings – before it was used and abused by twentieth century Nazi parties. It may even have been the swastika's association with good luck and purity which caused it to be adopted by Hitler as a representation of a so-called 'pure race'. He might however have had second thoughts had he known that a similar symbol was used in West Africa to decorate ceremonial cloth used particularly

---

DID YOU KNOW?

Swastika derives from three Sanskrit words: *su* meaning 'good' or 'well', *asti* 'to be' and *ka* 'making more/less'. Swastika therefore means roughly 'to be making better' not in the sense of recovery after illness, but improving the sort of person you are.

although not exclusively for funerals. Called *nkontim*, the symbol means 'loyalty', although its literal meaning is 'hair of the queen's servant' (see picture, below).

In heraldry the swastika's 'legs' are often truncated after the right angle, giving it the appearance of a straight leg with a foot on the end; the shape is often known as a fylfot. The heraldic name is something of a giveaway as it means 'four footed', as opposed to the triskelion's 'three legged'.

The shape's the thing

Although both sun cross and triskelion may be solar symbols they have an important and obvious difference. Sun crosses are usually circular and often bi-polar symmetrical, which means that each half reflects the other regardless of where the dividing line runs – think of a cross inside a circle. Some solar symbols, those where the legs are bent, are rotationally symmetrical, which means that they look the same when turned round; all the symbols on the opposite page are like this. Triskelia

Left: Manx flag at Union Mills
Below: Three Legs of Man in window
of Sefton Hotel, Harris Promenade, Douglas
Below left: Three Legs of Man plaque on wall of
Santon Motel, Main Road, Santon
Bottom: Three Legs of Man design on wall of
bungalow in Glen Road, Laxey

are *always* rotationally symmetrical and *never* bi-polar symmetrical, i.e., if you fold triskelia in half the two halves don't match, but if you turn triskelia round they continue to look the same. This is of course self evident if you look at them.

Although the triskelion has come to be associated with all sorts of mystical meanings – the Christian trinity, for example, or the link between birth, life and death – it may not have begun that way. We've all doodled in the margin of papers, or drawn squiggles in the sand, and the three legs makes an interesting shape, with all sorts of possibilities for adaptation. Perhaps seven thousand years ago some stone-age graphic designer sketched out the first triskelion and just liked the pattern it made.

THE THREE LEGS OF MAN

If no-one can be quite sure where the three-legged design comes from, we're equally unsure why it was adopted as the symbol for the Isle of Man. When the island came under Scandinavian rule its symbol, not surprisingly, was a Viking ship. The triskelion seems to have replaced the ship as the island's emblem around 1266, when Alexander III of Scotland gained control of the island, although both symbols may have been used earlier and both continued to be used concurrently for a while. In fact the Viking ship is still used occasionally: it forms the logo of publishers The Manx Experience and that of the Thanet Campaign for Real Ale for example, and was the marque of the Rover car. Although a potent symbol, there is little evidence that the Viking ship was a coat of arms in the strict sense however. Such is not the case for the Three Legs of Man. If the ship started as a symbol and segued into being used as a coat of arms, the three legs seems to have started as a coat of arms before being adopted as a ubiquitous symbol.

Several thirteenth-century heraldic manuscripts, including various Rolls of Arms, contain descriptions of the Three Legs of Man. The most complete is probably Walford's Roll compiled around 1275. It has two descriptions of the three legs device, the longest being: *Le Roy de Man, de goules a treys gambes armes o tutte le quisses et chek un cornere seyt un pee* (the King of Mann, red background, three armoured legs, the whole thighs, and each corner is a foot). The three-legged device for the King of Man seems to have been widely accepted by the mid thirteenth century, as another heraldic roll from 1280, now in the Fitzwilliam Museum in Cambridge, England, pictures it.

A version of the Viking ship used as the Isle of Man's emblem as it appears in the north window in Lonan Old Church

New management and a new logo

Magnus III was the last King of Norway also to style himself King of Mann. After trying – and failing – to take the island from him by force, the Scottish King, Alexander III, eventually purchased Mann from Magnus's successor. Magnus III had as his symbol a mailed leg, bent at the knee. Alexander's wife was sister to the King of Sicily, and the Sicilian flag has three naked legs with a face superimposed

Modern copy of the Three Legs of Man as they appear on a thirteenth century Roll of Arms

The Sicilian flag flying in a back garden in Ramsey

where the legs join (see also page 6). It seems at least possible that the two symbols were amalgamated in the Three Legs of Man.

At this point it's important to remember that people have always liked symbols and badges to identify themselves with their tribe or team; we would probably now call such a representative symbol a logo. Mediaeval fighting men were recognised by the pattern on their shield, the decoration on their helmet or sometimes by the design on a long cloth tabard worn on their body over their armour. Officially the patterns are called a device (on the shield), crest (on the helmet), and decoration on the surcoat (over the armour). Obviously it could be confusing if different people used the same symbol, so so-called coats of arms developed out of the wish to be clear about whom everyone was when faces were hidden inside helmets; combatants wouldn't want to kill their allies – or probably not. Heralds organised tournaments and therefore needed to be clear about identities, so they became experts at distinguishing the various armorial designs. Soon people began to check with the heralds before adopting a new picture to put on their armour, to make sure that no-one else was using it too. In this way a more formal method of deciding, agreeing and designing coats of arms was born.

Formal identification

A symbol or logo has always been relatively informal and still is. A coat of arms is quite another matter, and most people know that you can't just make one up and decide to use it, or at least not officially. Coats of arms are granted by letters patent, which means that the crown has to agree them. They can be granted to individuals or corporate bodies but never to a family or name. Only one person can hold a coat of arms at a time – obviously when you remember that they were intended to identify individuals – and the right to use a particular coat of arms is inherited, usually through the male line. Coats of arms

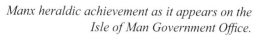

Manx heraldic achievement as it appears on the Isle of Man Government Office.

DID YOU KNOW?

Strictly speaking the term 'coat of arms' refers only to the shield, also called an escutcheon. When the shield appears as part of a display of all the honours to which the owner is entitled - crown, supporters, motto, etc., the whole is called an 'heraldic achievement'.

may have close similarities between family members, but each is unique.

There are two kinds of differences – differencing is an heraldic term and self explanatory – those belonging to sons, and those belonging to other members of the family. In the former case the difference is made either by adding a different border (the Scottish system) or by superimposing a cadency mark (the English system, called such from the word 'cadet' meaning a young man) for each son. When the father dies, the eldest son inherits the coat of arms and can remove the label which has distinguished his coat of arms while his father was alive (younger sons retain their difference marks and pass them down to their descendants). Members of other branches of an extended family who are unlikely to inherit the original coat of arms may have a coat of arms of their own which alludes to it but with important differences. An easy way to see how differencing works is to look at the coats of arms for the British royal family.

The heraldic achievement of Peter de Tremayne

'Tailors' for coats of arms

Today the College of Arms is the authority for everything to do with heraldry for England, Wales, Northern Ireland and much of the Commonwealth. Not for Scotland however; that responsibility is held by the Court of the Lord Lyon.

The Court of the Lord Lyon came into being in the fourteenth century (the College of Arms was founded a century later in 1484), so did not exist formally when Alexander III took over Mann. In 1418 however, Henry V issued a writ to some English sheriffs to the effect that no-one could decide to use a coat of arms unless they'd either inherited it or been granted it by the crown, so the English king was obviously taking the question of formal identification seriously. Heraldry had existed since the eleventh century, as did the heralds themselves with their specialist knowledge, so it's at least possible that Alexander III contacted them with ideas about a more formal device to represent his new acquisition.

The fact that he may have done so is suggested by another coat of arms granted around that time. Cornwall might at first seem a long way from both the Isle of Man and Scotland, but by sea the distance is not so far. The Cornish are Celts and the Cornish language is close to both Manx and Scots Gaelic. Peter de Tremayne was a Cornish nobleman, possibly a Templar Knight, and one of the commanders in the army of Edward I of England, the most powerful ruler in the surrounding islands at the time. Edward had been in Sicily, in 1272, landing there on his way back from the ninth and last crusade.

Not only did he visit Sicily, it was there that he learned of the death of his father Henry III, and that he himself had become Edward I of England. Less than a year later Tremayne was granted the right to a coat of arms. The Tremayne device is what is known as canting arms or a rebus, which means that it was a visual pun, in this case of the family name. *Trois mains*, is French for 'three hands', and the Tremayne coat of arms is three right arms, bent at the elbow, joined in a triskelion and on a red background (see previous page). It is almost exactly the same as the Manx emblem except using arms instead of legs.

The Three Legs of Man as one of the panels in a frieze around the top of the Manx Museum building (left) and on Amberley House, Windsor Road (below). Both are in Douglas and within 100 yards of each other. Each is an accurate, if black and white representation of the Three Legs, but they still manage to be totally unalike

Networking was just as important in the fourteenth century as it is today and Edward I and Alexander III certainly knew each other, even if they didn't get on. (Edward I was also known as the Hammer of the Scots, which suggests a stormy relationship with the Scottish king, to say the least.) Even so, if you're a king or even merely a member of the nobility, your peer group is very small and, with intermarriages, everyone tends not only to know everyone else, but also to be related. Alexander may therefore have known Perys Tremaen as Peter de Tremayne was sometimes called – at the time spelling was largely a matter of choice. There is no proof but surely the appearance and timing of the three legs of the Isle of Man and the three arms of Tremayne can't be entirely unrelated.

How to get it looking right

Interestingly, once a coat of arms has been granted, it is not a picture in the letters patent which decides what the arms should look like, but the concise verbal description of them. The original idea was that the description, known as a blazon from the French *blason* meaning 'shield', provided instructions for anyone wanting to paint the coat of arms on any property owned by the holder of the arms. In the mediaeval period, every nobleman would have kept his own household, which would have included illustrators and painters, and they would do whatever painted decoration was necessary. It's quicker, easier (and cheaper in paint) to describe the device rather than sketch it. Today the blazon for a new coat of arms is still written in a pseudo French developed from the Norman French in use when heraldry was first formalised. Brevity, word order and exactness are very important to avoid confusion, which means that, to modern and non-expert readers, a blazon is usually completely mystifying.

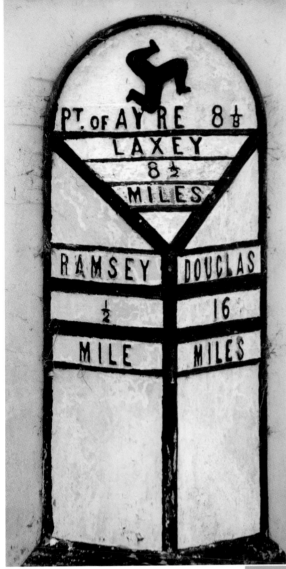

The blazon for the Three Legs of Man is: *gules three legs embowed conjoined in the fess point in armour proper argent garnished and spurred or* (see what I mean?!). The Manx description for its arms (or legs) is much simpler: *ny tree cassyn* (the three legs).

In everyday language the blazon for the Manx device describes a red background (*gules*) on which are three bent (*embowed*) legs joined together at the hip, in silver (*argent*) armour with spurs and other decorations of gold (*or*). Because it is the description and not a picture which determines what the coat of arms looks like, there can often be quite a bit of leeway in the different representations of it, all of which can nevertheless be correct.

The shape is obviously the most striking part of the design, but it might be worth briefly considering the colours of the coat of arms. Red, as the colour of blood, tends to symbolise life, but can also represent fire, passion, war and danger. Because of the way our eyes work, red is one of the easiest colours to see. 64% of the specialist cells in our eye are adapted literally to seeing red; try taking a photograph with something red in it and see how it stands out. Silver and gold, as precious metals, obviously represent wealth, but gold also represents the sun and is, in addition a very easy colour to see. The simplicity of the design, and the colours used to represent it make the Three Legs of Man both striking and highly symbolic.

Milestone on the Ballure Road just outside Ramsey. Note the distance to Point of Ayre. How many other signposts do you know which give distances to one eighth of a mile?!

Street lamps in Douglas

As the blazon of a coat of arms is what actually defines it, it's always interesting to note what the description does *not* say. In the case of the Three Legs of Man, for example, the official description doesn't say which way the legs should be pointing, nor how much the knees should be bent. Consequently any arguments about what is right in these respects is a matter of tradition rather than correctness. In fact some representations of three legs are manufactured as cut out shapes and can therefore be viewed from both sides, with the legs 'running' in either direction (see picture of street lamps on previous page).

What are the legs wearing?

Armour of course, but what sort of armour? The blazon describes only armour with spurs and does not specify the sort. As the blazon specifies spurs then the original armour was obviously that of a horseman – no great surprise when the only people likely to have wanted shield devices in the first place expected them to identify mounted nobility. Nowadays one set of armour looks very much like another to most laymen, but it was not always so. From the heraldic point of view, the earliest form of armour was mail, often called chainmail; armour had existed earlier of course, but formalised coats of arms had not. Consequently the earlier depictions of the three legs device shows the legs wearing chainmail with a single spur.

One of the oldest known reproductions of the Three Legs of Man appears on the Maughold cross, now inside Maughold Church, dating from the fourteenth century

Mail worked well against blows from swords and clubs, but was less successful at deflecting or protecting against piercing. During the thirteenth century, after the development of impact weapons with greater kinetic energy (more 'oomph' to you and me) such as longbows, lances and crossbows, plate armour began to supplement and then, by the fifteenth century, to replace chainmail. Heraldic artists would depict what was most familiar to them, so later renditions of the Three Legs of Man tend to show them wearing plate armour with roweled spurs. Rather than the long 'sock' of mail worn by earlier legs, the later legs are depicted wearing greaves over the calf and ankles, poleyns over the knee cap and cuisses to protect the thigh. They still do so today.

At the risk of being frivolous, the wording of the blazon, saying 'armour' as it does, wouldn't exclude the legs wearing something like a bomb disposal suit or cricketing pads, although either would look rather odd with spurs.

Three Legs of Man relief, beautifully painted, on the wall of a house on Ballure Road, Ramsey

Clockwise or anti?

An old adage described the three legs as kneeling to England, turning their back on Ireland and kicking Scotland. Nowadays it's very rare to see depictions of the three legs kneeling to anyone (and quite right too!). Except to those arriving at Ronaldsway of course… (see picture, right). There has, however, been a lot of discussion about which way the legs should be 'running', clockwise or anticlockwise.

To start with, the terms 'clockwise' or 'counterclockwise' have of course only been in use since the invention of clocks. Clocks with dial faces similar to those we are familiar with today were invented around the fourteenth century. The earlier terms were 'sunwise' for clockwise, i.e. the direction in which the sun travels through the sky (at least in the northern hemisphere), and 'widdershins' from the Middle High German *wider* (against) and *sinnig* (sensible) meaning in an opposite direction to normal, i.e. anticlockwise. Obviously moving in a direction contrary to that of the sun was inadvisable if your religion was one

of those which venerated it.

In Scotland, turning sunwise, i.e. clockwise, was considered luckier than the alternative, so it may be that the original design introduced by the King of Scotland, Alexander III, showed the legs running clockwise, i.e. with the point of the bent knee facing to the right. Druids were said always to walk clockwise around their holy places, as do Buddhists and Hindus. Up to at least the beginning of the last century, it was considered unlucky in Britain to walk anticlockwise around a Christian church, even though in the Eastern Orthodox Church the exact opposite was true.

Clockwise would therefore seem to be the preferred way. But there is a problem. The three legs were originally designed primarily as a shield device, remember. Shields are worn on the left arm. If you have three legs running clockwise on a shield carried on the left, it looks as though the legs are running away – not a stunningly good advertisement for the wearer's prowess! There is an argument therefore for the three legs on a shield to run anticlockwise. On Mann, the oldest reproductions known of the three legs symbol appear on the Maughold cross (see opposite), dating from the fourteenth century, and on the Manx Sword of State dating probably from the fifteenth. In both cases the three legs are running anticlockwise.

Bryan Rudd, Bass Drummer, Ellan Vannin Pipes & Drums

19

On the other hand, a fifteenth-century carved image of the Three Legs of Man which appears in Manchester Cathedral, England show the legs as running clockwise (see right). James Stanley, younger brother of Thomas Stanley, King of Mann, became warden of the Collegiate Church in Manchester, now the cathedral, in 1481-2, which is why the Three Legs of Man appear in central England. Another representation and for similar family reasons appears above the nave in Beverley Minster in Yorkshire, and on the Derby Tomb in the parish church in Ormskirk; the Stanleys were also the Earls of Derby and the tomb was originally in Burscough Priory.

Other factors complicate matters further. For example, the biggest reproduction of the Three Legs of Man in the world is, fittingly, on the front of the biggest water wheel in the world, the Lady Isabella in Laxey (see picture, left). There the legs run clockwise. However they are cast iron, which means they were poured into a mould rather like a huge version of a jelly mould, with molton iron taking the place of the jelly. The mould would have been designed with the legs running anticlockwise. The mould carver would certainly have recognised that his work meant that the finished product would have been a reverse or mirror image of the mould, i.e. running clockwise. However, did the man who commissioned the work and who lacked the carver's experience also realise this?

Fifteenth century carving on end of choir stall, Manchester Cathedral. The three legs appear on a shield on the lower half. On the upper half is carved the Stanley symbol of the bird and bantling (eagle and child).
Photograph © Dominic Strange

Sometimes the three legs are shown running different ways on the same building. Here the legs appear above the entrance to the Manx Museum; compare the direction to those on page 16

It is even possible that the clockwise/anticlockwise distinction might have been one of the ways of differentiating the coats of arms of different members of the same family, which we discussed earlier (see page 15). It's unlikely, but possible.

In truth there isn't a correct way for the legs to run, and which way they are depicted is a matter of personal choice, tradition and custom. The motto *quocunque jeceris stabit* (whichever way you throw him he shall stand) is therefore even more apt.

The alternative history

Folklore also has its traditions as to the origin of the three legs. Legend has it that Manannan, the island's traditional protector, turned himself into a three-legged fiery hoop to roll down from North Barrule and rout invaders. A hoop of fire also figured in the midsummer revelry of Viking settlers celebrating the life of Baldr. According to Norse mythology Baldr was the son of Odin and Frigg, was famed for his

The Manx are proud of their flag and display it often
Above: the plaque on the roof of Laxey flour mill, Laxey.
Below: flying above Castle Rushen, Castletown

*Right: along Laxey Promenade
Below: Michael ('Mo') and Julie Owen about
to take part in sidecar trials near Dreemskerry
Bottom: boat house in memory of
William White on Garwick beach*

goodness, peace and joy, and was associated with the beneficial effects of the sun. Baldr's life culminated at midsummer, during which fires were lit to represent his funeral pyre. Hoops of fire were rolled down the hillside to symbolise the sun's decline – and we're back to sun crosses and the sun/fire origins of the Three Legs of Man again (see chapter 1).

Another legend claims the triskelion to be a representation of what we should now know as a flying saucer. Back in the time of the Druids some fishermen were driven ashore by a storm and set up camp on an unspecified Manx beach. As they were huddled around their fire, a huge fiery wheel supported on three armoured legs emerged from the stormclouds. It hovered above them in the mist before floating up the cliff and inland. The seaman took the apparition to be an omen of their escape and the three mailed legs became a lucky symbol thereafter.

Whatever the origin of the Three Legs of Man, they have today become a proud symbol of a fiercely independent nation. As such they appear all over the place and in all sorts of styles.

THREE LEGS EVERYWHERE!

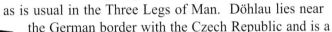

Many people do not know that the symbol of the Three Legs of Man, although rare, is not unique to the island. The Rabensteiner family of Döhlau in Bavaria, Germany had exactly the same emblem on its coat of arms; the blazon (see page 16-7) is: *drei im Dreipass gestellte geharnischte silberne Beine auf rotem Grund* (three armoured silver legs placed in a trefoil on a red ground). The family first started using the three-legged device around 1353, about 100 years after the Isle of Man adopted it. The family appears to have died out in the middle of the seventeenth century, but the three legs still make up part of the coat of arms of the municipality of Döhlau (see picture, right). The civic 'legs' are standing on the flat of one of the feet, although the Rabensteiner family 'legs' are running with pointed toes as is usual in the Three Legs of Man. Döhlau lies near the German border with the Czech Republic and is a small but pretty village, largely agricultural, with about half the population of Ramsey but covering an area about the size of Douglas.

In addition to the Manx coat of arms, and that of Rabensteiner/Döhlau, a three-legged symbol, although lacking clothing, occurs in the flag of Sicily (see page 14) and in the coat of arms of the town of Füssen, Germany near the Austrian border (see picture, left). Although both are in Bavaria, Döhlau and Füssen are about 260 miles apart, so the two symbols seem unlikely to be connected. Füssen means 'feet' in German so the flag is obviously a rebus or heraldic pun on the name of the town. There is also some indication that one of the old German shoemaking guilds in Mashau Bohemia (now Mastov, Czech Republic) may have used three conjoined legs as their coats of arms.

Not only legs

Triskelia lend themselves rather well to inclusion within coats of arms, because the shape of the shield is roughly triangular. Because of this, triskelia which have no connexion with the Three Legs of Man can sometimes look very like them. The coat of arms of the Polish family Rola, later used for the town and municipality of Modliborzyce, Poland, is a good example. On a red background and with a device of three scythe blades – the countryside is very flat and noted for its rich pasture – joined in the middle at a silver rose (see next page), the emblem is very reminiscent of the Manx three legs and has absolutely no connexion with it at all!

A triskelion of bugel horns is used as a coat of arms by many Polish families and the Vikings used the design of the triple horn of Odin (see page 8), but again there seems to be nothing to show that there is any connexion. It's

---

DID YOU KNOW?

A three-legged symbol appears as part of the late thirteenth century wall decoration of Karja Church on Saaremaa Island in Estonia (interestingly, Saaremaa's coat of arms is a Viking ship – see page 13). The shape painted in red on the wall of the church is the three-legged symbol, running clockwise. Each leg is the same shape, but decorated differently.

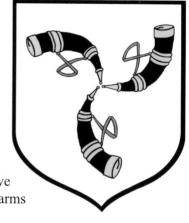

much more likely that sounding horns, i.e. horns that make a noise rather than those you drink out of, were important to both cultures as well as being a simple and striking shape to use as a device. The Polish heraldic system does not work in the same way as the British systems, and different families may use the same device. In this way several towns and administrative areas in Poland, including Dukla and Zakliczyn have the same or very similar coats of arms (see picture, right).

Modern – or not?

Less rare are three-'legged' symbols which are stylised triskelia and which are similar to the three legs of Man only in the pattern they make. The tri-spirals used on the millennium stone at St John's are such, as is the logo of Manx petroleum, and even the seal of the US Department of Transportation. It's possible that the designers of the logos intended to provide a stream-lined triskelion and were unaware that they were actually reverting to an earlier form (see chapter 1).

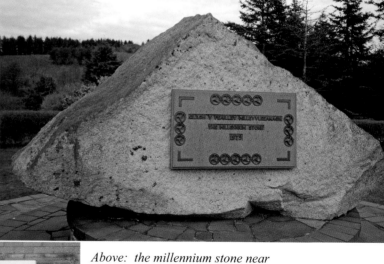

Above: the millennium stone near the arboretum at St John's
Left: the logo of Manx Petroleum and the Three Legs of Man on one of the company's buildings near the Battery Pier, Douglas

A similar effect using colour rather than line is used as the insignia of the Irish Air Corps (see picture, right). The corps was founded in 1924 and provides military air support to the Ireland's army and navy, as well as air medical services. The three colours are the same as on the Irish flag, where the green is said to represent the Gaelic tradition, the orange the followers of William of Orange and the white the peace between them. Japanese tomoe (see page 7) look similar and are often used with the same symbolism in the Shinto religion.

Another ancient variation on the theme of triskelia is the valknut (see page 9), which appears to be a set of three interlaced triangles. The ancient device forms the logo of Ellen Vannin Fuels (EVF – see picture, left). It's a clever interpretation as the three triangles, with a bit of squinting, can be seen to represent the initial letters of the name.

If spaced out a little, the three triangles can also look like three sevens, and it was three sevens which were used to form the triskelion which became the symbol of the Afrikaner Weerstandsbeweging (Afrikaner Resistance Movement

– see picture, left). The group was formed on 7 July 1973 and claims that the three sevens oppose the three sixes which the Biblical book of Revelations state is the number of the anti-Christ. Whether intended or not, the flag of the far right group of white separatists obviously echoes the Nazi swastika in shape and colour.

A more understandable use of a jagged line triskelion is the three bolts of lightning which make up the logo for the old Manx Electricity Authority (MEA).

Trying triquetras

We discussed in chapter 1 the possibility that the shape of the three legs might have derived from the centre of a triquetra (see page 9), and the knot makes one of the more elegant triskelia. It appears frequently in the Celtic knotwork which adorns many of the Manx crosses, and could even be said to be the basis of them.

Manx Electricity Authority van at Ramsey
during an extremely *high tide*

Because the design is attractive, simple, and yet compact it continues to be very popular. Archibald Knox based many of his world-famous designs on Celtic knotwork and, fittingly, at least one memorial plaque to him is decorated with the triquetra.

Triquetras appear to be a rope or line with no beginning and no end. Occasionally known as a trinity knot they have gained a lot of three-in-one symbolism and come to represent various spiritual ideas. Christians, for example, see the triquetra as representing the trinity, while some modern pagans consider that it represents the division of the world into land, sea

Plaque at the corner of Athol Street and Peel Road, Douglas

and sky. It's used in a secular context too; the far-left political party Scottish Republican Socialist Movement include a triquetra in their flag to represent past, present and future.

> **DID YOU KNOW?**
>
> The Chinese philosophy of yin and yan, represented by two 'comma' shapes fitted together inside a circle, states that apparent opposites are actually complementary. Although the shape looks similar to many triskelia, the thinking behind it is very different.

Not quite universal

One possible reason why triskelia weren't used even more widely, is that the pattern is very difficult to weave into cloth. Being three legged and therefore triangular, rather than four legged and therefore square, the triskelion does not lend itself to the warp and weft of weaving. Isle of Man Transport had a go at producing a triskelion on its upholstery with rather odd results. Even common forms of embroidery, for example cross stitch, or the ubiquitous tent stitch of tapestries, would be difficult to use to transfer a three-legged design onto cloth. A knight's surcoat (see page 14), although made of cloth, would often have had the device painted rather than embroidered onto it – surcoats tended to get torn and muddy (and bloody) very quickly. A triskelion's lack of bi-polar symmetry wouldn't therefore have mattered. For tapestries designed to last,

The Three Legs of Man on a house overlooking Laxey harbour

Above: entrance to Ballasaig Farm looking over Maughold. Ballaterson Farm is on the opposite hillside on the left (see front cover)
Right: weather vane on top of Pinfold Holiday Cottages, corner of New Road and Ballacollister Road, Laxey

however, a two-way symmetrical design would have been both simpler and quicker to reproduce. A fighting man may not have considered such, but his wife and her ladies would!

Today, with quicker forms of reproducing images, and more flexible materials to use, displaying your own version of the Three Legs of Man has never been easier. Many island residents do just that.

DID YOU KNOW?

Triskelion comes from the Greek *τρισκελής* (triskeles) made up of *τρι* (tri) meaning three and *σκέλος* (skelos) meaning leg.

ACKNOWLEDGEMENTS

I am indebted to several organisations and individuals who gave up their time to provide help, information and/or photographic material. They include, individuals: Christine Bull, Paul Davenport, Mary Gyseman, Michael and Julie Owen, Nick Pickford, Bryan Rudd, Breeshey Skillicorn, Dominic Strange and Claire Tuffy; and organisations: Ellan Vannin Pipes & Drums, Office of Public Works in Ireland, Peveril MCC and the Virgers of Beverley Minster (they really are spelt with an 'i').

Always of course I am grateful for the support and photographic expertise of my husband, George Hobbs.

Thank you all for your help and assistance; any mistakes are entirely mine.

Note: The title of this booklet, *Three Legs Good*, is a deliberate misquotation from George Orwell's *Animal Farm*, where the animals' maxim is 'four legs good'.

SELECTED BIBLIOGRAPHY

Oswald, H.R., *Vestigia Insulae Manniae Antiquiora or Armorial Bearings of the Isle of Man*, The Manx Society, 1860

The Journal of the Manx Museum, Vol VI, 1959-60, No. 76, article 'The Origin of the Arms of Man' by Anthony R. Wagner, Richmond Herald.

The Manx NoteBook; A Quarterly Journal of Matters Past and Present Connected with the Isle of Mann, Number 5 January 1886, A.W. Moore (ed), article 'The Armorial Bearings of the Isle of Man: their Origin, History and Meaning' by J. Newton

The Manx NoteBook; A Quarterly Journal of Matters Past and Present Connected with the Isle of Mann, Number 7 July 1886, A.W. Moore (ed), article 'Supplementary Note on the Armorial Bearings of the Isle of Man' by J. Newton

Proceedings of the Isle of Man Natural History and Antiquarian Society, Volume XII Number 2 April 2007-March 2009, Presidential address 'Heraldry in the Isle of Man: History, Practice, Jurisdiction and Self-Image' by Jonathan Kewley

Decorative brickwork on the public convenience, Bride